Ridiculous Liaisons

Ridiculous Liaisons

Gabriela Anaya Valdepeña

Edited by

Douglas James Martin

Darkness Visible Books

La Jolla   2011

First edition published in 2011 by

Darkness Visible Books
P.O. Box 577
La Jolla, CA 92038
darknessvisiblebooks@yahoo.com

Section One, "Sweet Cherry Simone," has appeared
separately in *The Espresso*, San Diego CA, John Rippo,
editor.

FIRST EDITION

Printed in the United States of America

Library of Congress Control Number: 2011926304

ISBN: 978-0-9774000-5-8

For Scott

Le ridicule qu'on a augmente toujours en proportion qu'on s'en défend.

—Laclos

CONTENTS

SWEET CHERRY SIMONE

Sweet Cherry Simone was betrothed
to a chef named Butch Bonmarito,
a stylish, but plain dealing, macho,
no insidious *chingaquedito*.

Nor was Butch some glib fancy talker;
he spoke from his gut, heart, and mind,
and the words that he whispered to Cherry
were unceasingly gentle and kind.

And yet woe to the cad who dared send
señorita an amorous query.
Bonmarito would suffer no fool
to make plays for his glamorous Cherry.

Poor Joe lost a favorite tooth.
Poor Al nursed a fractured left pinky.
Poor Beau was in bed for a week
after Butch kicked his impudent dinky.

But Barnaby Leghorn was neither
a foolish, nor forthright monsieur.
He was wealthy, and proud, and lascivious,
and a cunning, when crossed, saboteur.

So although he'd no interest in Spanish,
he enrolled in Simone's language school,
and paid extra for one-on-one tutoring,
from the *chica* who made his mouth drool.

"She's sure to soon fall for my money!
and as for the Spanish, who cares?"
Leghorn thought, as he licked his thin lips
and imagined her *sans* underwears.

He couldn't help it, she looked so damn good
in those flowery, feminine dresses,
as she flashed those glossy flash cards,
running fingers through long bouncy tresses!

Trouble is, though he claimed to be keen,
Cherry thought him a rather slow study.
"*Señor*, pay attention," she'd scold,
whence he'd scowl like a dull fuddy-duddy.

After weeks, Cherry saw no improvement.
Mr. Leghorn could not roll his *r*'s,
couldn't distinguish his fem'nine from masculine,
and committed innumerable *faux pas.*

He confused the noun *mono* with *mona*,
saying Cherry looked much like a monkey,
and he'd mix his past tense with his present.
until all conjugations went funky!

And despite the *dinero* he offered,
Cherry couldn't long endure the frustration.
"Mr. Leghorn," she said, "I must cease,
with regret, academic relations."

"But how dare you," Barnaby sputtered,
"scorn a man of my wealth and my stature!
I'll close down your school, little lass,
if you tempt my long-suffering nature!"

"*Señor*, please!" Cherry quickly retorted.
"Though you may very well own the town,
it's quite clear you can't grasp *español.*
You don't even know basic nouns!"

Her defiance sparked rage, and sparked lust.
Should he ruin or kiss this bold dame?
(Though with Barnaby's breath one might judge
that the two would be one and the same.)

But when Leghorn went in for the kill,
pursing tightly his thin, awkward lips
while closing his beady gray eyes,
a heavy clenched fist struck his ribs.

"Just what do you think you are doing?"
cried Butch, Cherry's boldhearted gallant.
"If you come near my woman again,
you'll learn more 'bout my prize-fighting talent!"

Just then, students poured from their classes,
and guffawed at the jabbering Leghorn,
who clutched his bruised torso, while swearing
that Butch would soon wish he weren't born.

"Bring it on; I'm not scared!" challenged Butch,
while maneuvering Leghorn outdoors.
"Oh thank God he is gone!" exclaimed Cherry,
"that bilious, insufferable bore!"

Later on, back at Butch's trattoria,
all the customers cheered the young pair,
since the lowdown on Leghorn's shellacking
had traveled like bolts through the air.

And when Leghorn's chauffeur sauntered in
to pick up a quick order to go,
they all snickered and taunted and booed,
'til he fled to inform the vile crow.

"This is war!" cried the rancorous Leghorn.
"She shall wish she had suffered my kiss."
Then he stroked at his cold, crooked pecker,
while he plotted, and snorted, and hissed.

"I know plenty of thugs," Leghorn mused,
"who, for a quite reasonable fee,
would kill, then dispose of a body,
or just Tanya Harding a knee.

"But then murder's too short-lived to savor,
and a beating is so déclassé,
and such fates would find much too much honor
in Simone's loving tears, anyway.

"It's their love that must needs be destroyed!
But just how should I pull that one off?"
Leghorn seethed, remembering the mocking
at Butch's esteemed feeding trough.

Then at last, Leghorn thought on the proverb—
how revenge is a dish best served cold.
He would wait for all passion to cool,
then destroy them just as he'd foretold.

And to murder such love with such coldness
would be hailed as a sovereign coup!
Thus Leghorn would need, for a span,
bid all passion and anger *adieu*.

A POLYGLOT FROM EL PASO

Some months later, sweet Cherry had nearly
forgotten that ass, when one morning
she arrived at her work to find chains
'round the door, and a sign saying: *WARNING*

THIS BUILDING HAS NOW BEEN CONDEMNED!
"But how could this be, Jesus Mary!
This place was restored up to code,
after grandpa bequeathed it to Cherry!

"Could it be I have termites, or mold?
Is the problem the fire escape?"
Cherry tried to besiege City Hall,
but was soon quite cocooned in red tape.

One by one she lost all of her students
to a new institute down the street
that had just opened up, unexpectedly.
It was christened *The World's Elite*,

and was owned by a woman named Margot,
a polyglot fresh from El Paso,
soon a frequenter of the trattoria,
though Butch *nunca le hizo caso.*

Then one day, while she dined all alone,
Margot suddenly choked on a shrimp,
and 'gan frantically waving for help,
like a streetwalker hailing her pimp.

Butch rushed to her table, at once,
thrusting strong hands under her sternum.
"Oh *grazie*," she cooed, with a hug,
marking collar with lipstick, and venom.

Next day, taking shirts to the cleaners,
Cherry noticed a strange shade of red
on an imprint of lips not her own,
and the doubts 'gan to spin in her head.

After all, Butch was gone so much lately.
He said he'd extended his hours,
just to pay for a sharp Philly lawyer
to help fight the municipal powers.

But she didn't want to question or nag.
"If he's cheating, I'll know soon enough,"
Cherry thought, "I could tell from his scent
if he's sniffing another chick's muff."

Meantime Margot could not get enough
of that down home Italian cuisine,
though you'd never guess that from her frame—
she was built like a star of the screen.

And after one Monday's lasagna,
Margot beckoned big Butch to come near,
for a chat, while she liberally sprayed
her favorite perfume in the air.

"I'm so sorry," she voiced, deep and breathy,
when her fragrance stung Butch's right eye.
"I just wanted to praise your fine pasta.
To say it's the best is no lie!"

"I'm so happy you like it," Butch smiled.
"You must make it a point to come back
Friday night, when our special's spaghetti."
Margot nodded, while jiggling her rack.

And that night, when she kissed Butch's temple,
Cherry noticed a fresh scent of musk.
"Did you buy yourself brand new shampoo?"
Cherry asked, trying not to sound brusque.

"No, baby, it's just plain ol' Suave,"
Butch responded, enjoying her touch.
"*Te gusta, mi linda*?" he teased.
"Not really," she frowned, "it's too much!"

Some days later, while dusting at Butch's,
Cherry answered a call from the florist,
confirming an order for roses
to be dropped off at Avenue Forest.

"My school's on that street," Cherry thought.
"Are those flowers intended for me?"
"What address?" Cherry asked of the clerk.
When he told her, she fell to her knees.

It belonged to that new language school!
"And to whom will they go?" Cherry probed.
"No last name," he replied, "just Margot."
Now poor Cherry lamented like Job!

But still, she must not jump the gun.
She should give Butch a chance to explain.
Could be Margot was just an old friend,
or a customer who had complained.

But the way Butch became so defensive
unsettled her nerves all the more.
He said Margot had sent him some business.
"She's a client, that's all!" her Butch swore.

"But flowers, especially roses—
such a common romantic device!"
said Cherry. "I'd like to believe you,
but some coupons would well have sufficed!"

At the very same time, back at Leghorn's,
Margot bragged to her confederate,
"So the seeds of discord have been planted,
without even kissing him yet!

"And when Butch sees my beckoning knockers,
plus these goodies, well that's all she wrote!"
Margot vowed, while uncrossing her legs,
Sharon Stone-ing before the old goat.

"And a partner makes plotting more fun,"
Margot smiled, slipping off her thin dress,
and moved closer, so Leghorn could grope her,
thus displaying surprising largesse!

A HANDSOME AND
WELL-DRESSED ATTORNEY

Poor Cherry! She didn't have the money
for lawyer, let alone plain-clothed dick,
to win back her building and school,
or to spy on her paramour's prick.

But one day, while she helped out at Butch's
a young man came to see Miss Simone,
a handsome and well-dressed attorney,
in a cloud of expensive cologne.

"I got word of your case," he explained,
"and my moniker's *Harvey R. Wood*.
You've been wronged, and you're owed compensation.
I'll see that the city makes good!"

"Who are you?" jealous Butch interrupted,
"This is *my* girl, and *my* restaurant."
"I'm Miss Cherry's new counsel," Wood quipped.
But then Cherry replied, "No you aren't.

"I mean, how could I possibly pay you?
I'm sure that you don't work for free."
"But let's say we could pay," Butch broke in.
"Just exactly what would be your fee?"

"Well, nothing up front," Wood replied.
"If we win, I'll just take ten percent."
"That sounds good to me," Cherry nodded;
but Butch still didn't trust the young gent.

"Got a card, mister mouthpiece?" he asked.
And when Wood gave his card to the gal,
Butch snatched it from Cherry's small hands,
and then sneered, "I'll be seeing you, pal."

Later on, Butch insisted she spurn
Harvey Wood's unsolicited offer.
But it's not like she had a real choice,
with no job, and an emptied out coffer.

And so Cherry defied her dear Butch,
retrieving Wood's card from the trash.
When she called him, Wood readily vowed,
"I will win back your school, plus cash!

"Shall we talk about this over dinner
and review all the court protocol?
You can tell your big friend not to worry—
I won't ply you with much alcohol."

But then Cherry confessed to her counsel
she had contacted him on the sly.
"Your palooka's quite over-protective,"
Wood remarked, "though I understand why!"

Well it took only two or three meetings
for Wood to lay out a clear case.
And despite Butch's sour consternation,
Cherry smiled to have hired an ace.

But why ask her to dinner so often,
to repeat things he'd already told?
And yet how could she really complain?
Wood was fun, and the meals, five-star gold!

And it certainly wouldn't profit Cherry
to decline Harvey Wood's invitations,
undermining the passion he needed
for tedious, long litigations.

After all, it was really just business,
like Butch himself swore, when he sent
all those flowers to Margot, instead
of instructing the bitch to get bent!

JUST BUSINESS

Meanwhile, back at Butch's trattoria,
the business was better than ever!
Margot sent him both teachers and students,
recommending the food with great fervor.

"It's no trouble," Marg said, when Butch thanked her.
"I'm happy to tout your place, hon.
But please keep in mind that my tongue
is unselfish in more ways than one!"

Margot's bold innuendo thrust Butch
immediately into a tizzy.
He tried to remember his Cherry,
but, nevertheless, remained dizzy.

Though when Cherry showed up to help out,
a fair vision in velvet and lace,
the thought of Marg sucking him off,
now inspired, not lust, but distaste.

Marg promptly rushed up to her rival,
saying "Hi, you must be little sister?"
"*Soy su novia, no su hermana!*"
Cherry sparked, reclaiming her mister.

"I would never have guessed," Margot smirked,
tow'ring tall over Butch's young Miss,
and, extending a cold hand to Cherry,
she was met with a glacial dis!

"Why so rude?" Butch asked Cherry, in private.
"Thanks to Margot, I'm doing so well!
I get business from all of her students,
and we're only good friends, can't you tell?"

"But she stole all those students from me!"
Cherry sadly shot back at her man.
"Now that lawyer could yet set it right.
But you're jealous; you don't understand!"

"I'm so sorry, my darling," Butch softened,
"I have been most unfair; you are right.
I tossed out Wood's card, but I'll find it,
and I promise to call him tonight."

But, naturally, Butch soon discovered
she'd already been meeting with Wood,
and his Cherry's deception cut deeper
than even his sharpest knife could.

And though Cherry implored his forgiveness,
Butch stubbornly scowled and brooded,
showing little regard for the fact
that her money tree, now, was denuded.

Nonetheless, Cherry soon got good news:
Harvey'd argued and threatened, and pleaded,
and pleaded, and threatened, and argued,
'til, at last, the city conceded.

"This calls for a fine celebration!"
Harvey cheered, asking Cherry to dine.
But Cherry was mindful of Butch
and chose to politely decline.

"I'll share the good news," Cherry planned,
"when Butch closes down at eleven."
But, when she showed up, he already
was bingeing, on Seven and Seven,

not alone, I might add, but with Margot!
Butch beckoned her close, with a grin,
but instead Cherry turned to the exit
and left them to choke on their gin.

"Now what did she want?" Margot quizzed.
"She's my sweetheart." Butch said. Margot frowned,
"Are you sure she's not hot on that lawyer?
I've been seeing them all over town."

"He's just working her case," Butch protested.
"Oh I bet he is," Margot now sassed.
"Don't compete with her." Butch remonstrated,
"You will find yourself sorely outclassed."

"Now listen here, Butch," she asserted,
"just what kind of friend would I be
if I lied to you 'bout your own girl?
I'm only the messenger, see."

"You must be confused, or mistaken,"
Butch replied. "My Cherry's no cheat."
"Whatever you say," Marg conceded.
Now how about something to eat?"

"My kitchen is closed," Butch lamented.
"But there's always *The Pancake Chateau*."
"I'm so famished!" Margot exclaimed,
and, grabbing his arm, barked "Let's go!"

"Well okay, but first I'll call Cherry.
She might want to catch up with us there."
But when only her voicemail responded,
Butch quietly began to despair.

And instead of *The Pancake Chateau*,
they communed at his bar, over drinks.
"Don't chase her," sly Margot advised.
"She'll come back when she's had time to think."

 "Now let's work on that smile," Margot teased,
"while I primp in the pink powder room."
Then she came back, smelling like Cherry—
She had put on the same damn perfume!

Poor Butch couldn't resist, so he kissed her,
then whispered, "*Mi ángel, te quiero.*"
Next he cupped her select, shapely ass,
'til she squealed "*Ay, papi, que cuero!*"

21

At last, slave to nostalgia, and lust,
he dropped trou', like they teemed with red ants.
But when Margot gazed back like a gorgon,
that scared him back into his pants!

"Oh come on baby," Margot now hissed.
"We've only just barely begun.
I'll freak you all night, like no other,"
she boasted. "Let's have us some fun!"

But Butch, now averting his eyes,
pushed her out as damn fast as he could,
too drunk, and too smitten with Cherry,
to lend this Medusa his wood.

Butch collapsed, and cried out: "I came close
to despoiling the crown of romances!
Oh I pray that my cherubim Cherry
can forgive me, and grant second chances!"

He thanked God he'd not finally faltered.
True, he had gotten hard for a second,
but he didn't turn completely to stone.
It was true love that saved him, he reckoned.

IT WAS LOVE

Butch crashed in his office 'til noon,
then rushed out to make up with his Cherry,
but by then she was lunching with Harvey,
talking business and making much merry!

"I guess I've still time,' Cherry nodded,
"to lure my old students back in."
"Why yes, with the money you've won,"
Harvey said, "you'll get by until then.

And besides, I'll be first to sign up,"
Harvey smiled. "Would you mind teaching me?"
"Why of course not!" Cherry responded.
"I'd be honored. The answer is *Si!*"

After lunch, they went straight to her school,
now dusty, and starved for fresh air.
Harvey sprang up the windows, proclaiming,
"It is yours, once again, Cherry dear!"

Overjoyed, Cherry gave him a hug,
but then blushed, pulling back when she felt
the excitement inflating in Wood,
and now fearing they'd mutually melt.

Harvey felt that strong chemistry, too,
but considered it good for his plan.
He was working more colorful angles
than Picasso, George Braque, or Cézanne.

Back at Leghorn's, meanwhile, Margot
was complaining, "I'd throw you a bone,
'cause I busted my ass to break Butch,
but I tell you, the man's made of stone."

"You dumb whore!" Leghorn squawked. "Now get out!
So Marg fucked him, collected her cash,
and then flew, the next day, back to Texas,
leaving Leghorn a terrible rash.

"Now what did that slut, Margot, give me?"
Leghorn moaned, as he picked at his breakfast,
and his prick, when the butler announced:
"Mr. Wood!" with extravagant bombast.

Leghorn sputtered and cursed, between scratches:
"That Wood best have news to report,
or I'll make sure the moron's disbarred;
he'll be banned from both high and low court!"

"Let him in," Leghorn ordered his help,
then asked Wood if he'd broken the bitch.
"Cherry's ripe for the taking," Wood boasted.
Leghorn laughed, and then snorted, then itched.

"How long will it take?" Leghorn queried.
"You're trying my patience already."
"But I have a method," Wood countered,
"unlike Margot, so rash and unsteady.

"She screwed up where I'm sure to succeed.
In good time I will win Miss Simone.
And when she is mine, I will crush her,
then smile, as she's slowly undone."

"We've our own *Liaísons Dangereuses*"
Leghorn rubbed his cold talons together,
imagining himself like Valmont,
both good-looking and wickedly clever.

And, indeed, Leghorn might have been right.
There were none quite so cunning and cruel—
notwithstanding his minor misjudgement
in choosing Margot as his tool.

For though Marg was a maladroit cunt,
as the great Raymond Chandler once said—
it takes only one drop of suspicion
to poison an amorous bed.

And he'd already fixed it so Cherry
wouldn't even accept Butch's calls,
let alone open doors when he knocked.
Oh, how she was busting his balls!

Wood and Leghorn now rushed to place bets
on how soon Cherry'd falter, then fall,
though admitting 'twas no simple feat
to drill clear through a tempered steel wall!

But then that was the point, they agreed:
to break an unbreakable love!
Though perhaps they were both selling short
the devotion 'tween Butch and his dove.

26

For Butch couldn't stop aching for Cherry,
He would grimace whenever she'd tweet
she was out again, lunching with Harvey.
Just how many times must they meet?

He might have to postpone his "I'm sorry"
until he could catch her *sans* Wood.
Then he'd win, once again, his Maid Marion
with the dash of a new Robin Hood!

And, during this time, Butch reflected
on his weakness, and on his mistakes,
on the wasted time flirting with Margot,
on his tardiness slamming the brakes.

And he grew to especially regret
how, when Cherry caught him with Margot,
he didn't stop her from running away,
but kept drinking, and just let her go!

And perhaps after all, all those times
that he knocked on his Cherry's closed door
with no answer, she really was working
long nights at her school, like before.

And even if she lay in Wood's arms,
it's because he had driven her there!
How could he have lost such a woman,
so soulful, so sweet, and so fair?

It didn't matter how long it might take,
come hell or come Beatles reunion!
He'd give up on his Cherry when science
found a rabbit's foot stuck in the Cambrian!

So as soon as Butch heard from a patron
that Cherry was now back in business,
he rushed to make most of the chance
to embrace his victorious mistress,

finding Cherry in a one-on-one lesson
between her and that vile crustacean,
her fingers 'round Harvey's big mouth,
helping out with his pronunciation.

"*Muy bien, Señor Wood*!" she applauded.
"You're certainly catching on fast!"
"It's not me," he replied, "it's the teacher.
Spanish lessons with you are a blast!"

Butch stomached the whole conversation
while listening outside the door,
and resisting the urge to seize Wood,
then slam his glib yap 'gainst the floor!

Wood was gone soon enough, and then Butch
had his Cherry, at last, to himself,
to accept his bilingual "I'm sorry,"
then his *besos*, then everything else.

"Hello, Cherry," Butch tenderly greeted.
"Well hello, Butch," she coldly replied,
though she knew, from his eyes, that her Butch
was contrite, and now empty of pride.

On his knees, Butch expounded to Cherry,
how his love for her made it so easy,
in the end, to repudiate Margot,
how the thought of that slut made him queasy!

And Butch promised that, though he'd been tempted,
he'd remained ever-faithful to her.
Freaky winds had endeavored, but failed
to blow over the restaurateur.

Then he drew Cherry into his arms,
with a kiss, nullifying his sins,
their hearts now rehearsing together,
like Vivaldi's harmonious violins.

STEP UP HIS GAME

Now that Cherry and Butch had made up,
and their ardor was deeper than ever.
Wood needed to step up his game
if he were to secure his endeavor.

So Harvey enrolled in more classes,
and gazed at *novelas* at home,
making notes on new words, and new ruses,
to impress, or to trap, Miss Simone.

"Well you've certainly made an impression!"
 Cherry praised. "You're my best student yet!"
While Wood mused, "I'll soon flip the tortilla!
It is *you* who will soon be my pet."

And yet Cherry couldn't help liking Harvey.
Why in no time he seemed a dear friend!
(And a friend with hypnotic blue eyes,
plus a taut, and a perky, rear end!)

Moreover, Wood's fluency proved
a real boon for Simone's language school
(points that Harvey would try to exploit
to make Cherry a slave to his tool).

And even though Butch would still snarl
when she happened to mention Wood's name,
he wouldn't whine on and on, like before,
in an endless, exhausting refrain.

Truth is Cherry quite pitied poor Harvey.
His one interest seemed to be Spanish,
with no friends, nor a girl of his own.
So why not set him up with a Danish

instructor who worked at her school—
a leggy, young strawberry blond?
Cherry crossed all her fingers and prayed
that sweet Inga and Harvey would bond.

But next day, when she asked 'bout the date,
Inga wailed, "Harvey only one subject!
He not let me talk nothing of me.
His affection is only one object;

"Harvey only make fuck with Miss Cherry!"
"We're just friends," Cherry gasped, and then pleaded
with Inga, "Give Wood one more chance!"
(Hoping one would be all that was needed.)

But Harvey ignored Inga's offer
that he make a renewed first impression.
He was thinking that now was the time
to make Cherry a passionate confession!

The next night Cherry found she was free;
Butch was running the bar until two
on behalf of a Baptist convention.
He was sure to sell plenty of brew!

And so Cherry accepted Wood's offer
of some Thai food, after his lesson.
She was thinking she'd give him advice
on tapping Dane ass he was missing.

But Wood scoffed at her sage booty counsel,
pleading, "Cherry, I give you my word,
No soy nada tonto. I am not
some innocent, bumbling nerd.

"I just don't really fancy that Dane.
Why I don't even fancy the sluts
at the strip bar, near where that school
of Margot's once was, that got shut."

 "And just how did you come to know Margot?"
Cherry asked, quite naturally curious.
"Oh I took a few classes from her,"
Wood responded, cunningly spurious.

"And what's that about stripper pole sluts?"
Cherry added, then shrugged, "Never mind.
It is not my concern who you see,
who you call for a quick bump and grind."

"Now she's jealous," Wood smiled to himself.
Yes, it seemed things were starting to turn.
There'd be no better time to blurt out—
"You're the goddess who makes my heart burn!"

Harvey sounded so pained and sincere,
much as if he had truly been struck
by Cupid's hot barb, though with Wood
love had never before had such luck.

34

Cherry couldn't help but picture herself
in Wood's loyal and passionate arms.
And the thought didn't repulse her at all.
Wood was not a man lacking in charms.

But her Butch somehow knew that her heart
craved someone both sweet and aggressive.
Butch was safe, barring further discovery
of strange hairs or a perfumed missive.

So Cherry, at last, took Wood's hand,
"I'm not happy to see your heart breaking,
but I cannot accept these attentions;
you must know I am already taken."

"I shall simply, then, treasure your friendship,"
Harvey vowed, now feigning concession.
"Count on me, though, if Butch makes you cry,
or commits yet another transgression."

Back at home, Harvey paced his apartment.
His initial designs had been vexed
by sweet Cherry's frustrating fidelity.
What stratagem could he try next?

"If her heart is a safe," Harvey swore,
"it is one I'm devoted to cracking.
And I'll also make sure that her man,
Bonmarito, secures a good whacking.

"Then again, should I bother with Butch?
To lose Cherry'd be worse than a beating,
and he'll die when he finds that she left him
for a man whose affections prove fleeting.

"Poor Butch will return to her side
to discover her body and soul
died, too, when I left her, so coldly
repeating, 'It's beyond my control.'

"But can't dump her until I first win her!
Just how will I plunder that prize?
I could plant a red hair on his pillow,
or a forged *billet doux* by her eyes.

"But such proof is too easy to plant!
And a heart that is won in such fashion
wouldn't return me the requisite pleasure
when it's time for some tender heart smashing!

"Well then maybe I'll go for 'refined'—
read her sonnets by Vincent Millay,
take her out to hear Erik Satie,
make full use of both cash and cachet.

"Better yet, like her Butch, I'll be *macho*,
like in all those *novelas* I've viewed.
I'll just grab her, and kiss her, and claim,
'*eres mía*, and I am your dude!'"

So one night, without warning, in class,
Wood kissed Cherry, in mid conjugation.
And she let him, at first, but pulled back
before she achieved full elation.

"Please don't do that again," she entreated.
"This heart cannot live split in two."
"Nor can mine," whimpered Wood, "so choose *me*.
You must know I'm the best one for you."

"No, Harvey," she said, "I'm so sorry,
But my kisses are only for Butch.
You will find your own woman someday
who will love only you, and your touch."

"But you merit much better than Butch!"
Harvey cried, "I must tell you the truth.
Why remain so attached to a man
that you joined in the folly of youth?"

"But how," Cherry asked, "could my heart
ever put into words why it beats
por sólo un hombre?" Poor Harvey
knew nothing was left, but retreat.

WHO'S THE SCHLEP?

Now when Harvey reported to Leghorn
Cherry's heart was not yet up for grabs,
the bad news made our Leghorn still madder
than when Margot had loaned him the crabs.

"You're incompetent, weak, and a liar!
You promised me certain results!"
bellowed Leghorn to Wood, at his office.
"You're a schlep, and a dolt, and a klutz!

"Is it that hard to take down a slut?"
"Now you shut your damn mouth," Harvey warned,
"Miss Simone is no *mujerzuela*.
And you're just a creep who's been scorned!"

But as soon as he blurted that out,
Harvey froze in mid-thought, with a start.
He could scarcely believe his own words.
He could scarcely believe his own heart.

"Since when do I bother," Wood wondered
"to defend the good name of my prey,
when my only concern for Miss Cherry
is to fuck her, then throw her away?"

But he pictured her crying and broken
He couldn't help that it made his heart sick.
For some reason he wanted her happy.
For some reason he felt like a prick.

All that time he had spent with his victim,
conspiring as hard as he could
had backfired. He hadn't won Cherry.
It was Cherry's sweet soul had won Wood!

And now, as he mused on her patience,
on her laughter, and lovely accent
his lips trembled, in a bitter-sweet smile,
while Leghorn looked on, with contempt—

"Yes, I should have known," sputtered Leghorn,
"you'd become way too soft with that cunt.
Just look at you now, lovesick squirrel!
You told me you knew how to hunt!"

"You son of a bitch!" Harvey howled.
"I told you to watch your foul mouth!"
Harvey swung with clenched fist at his teeth,
knocking some of them north, and some south.

Then he punched Leghorn's nose, for good measure,
first sending the tip pointing west,
then, like a broke compass, back east,
while the blood flooded down Leghorn's chest.

"Bring it on!" Leghorn wailed through the gore.
"An old fighter can't unlearn his craft.
Now put up your dukes, you vile coward!"
But Harvey just stood there, and laughed.

Poor Leghorn was no match for Harvey.
He tried to punch back, but misstepped,
and then crashed through his own picture window.
"Who now," Wood inquired, "is the schlep?"

Leghorn cursed, and kept trying to get up,
though he'd broken both legs and both arms,
while Wood turned his thoughts back to Cherry,
remembering her kindness and charms—

"I could never deserve such an angel,
not after I plotted her fall.
But nor could I have hurt her," Wood realized.
"I'm no Vicomte Valmont, after all!"

LOLLING IN BED

Some weeks later, while lolling in bed
Butch and Cherry were cooing and chatting
"Guess who I ran into" Butch teased,
"while I was out thissing and thatting?"

"I can't ever imagine," said Cherry.
"You remember that strange Leghorn fucker?"
"Oh gross," she replied, "and where was he?"
"Near the booze store, by 6th street and Tucker."

"Did he recognize you?" Cherry frowned.
"I don't think so, he couldn't turn his head.
He was bandaged from neck to his toes
looking much like a mummy long dead!"

"I wonder what happened?" asked Cherry.
"I don't know, but you never will guess
who was pushing his chair. That slut Margot!
Must be helping the fool convalesce."

"And I didn't even know they had met!"
Cherry wondered. "Though it's no surprise
that two assholes would end up together.
After all, doesn't shit attract flies?"

"And speaking of your former students,"
Butch added, "what happened to Wood?"
I thought him a huckster at first,
but I guess, in the end, he made good.

"Yes, it's true, Harvey won back my school,"
but it's weeks since I've seen him at all.
Though a note said he cherished my classes,
and was glad to help fight city hall.

He said I was the best of his teachers,
and he'd learned to see life through new eyes,
but thought now he'd best practice his Spanish
in Ixtapa, beneath its blue skies."